Open *the*
Windows
of
Heaven

© 2013 by Barbour Publishing, Inc.

Written and compiled by Sabrina McDonald.

Print ISBN 978-1-62416-691-4

eBook Editions:
Adobe Digital Edition (.epub) 978-1-62836-315-9
Kindle and MobiPocket Edition (.prc) 978-1-62836-316-6

Scripture quotations marked KJV are taken from the King James Version of the Bible.

Scripture quotations marked NASB are taken from the New American Standard Bible, © 1960, 1962, 1963, 1968, 1971, 1972, 1973, 1975, 1977, 1995 by The Lockman Foundation. Used by permission.

Scripture quotations marked NLT are taken from the *Holy Bible*. New Living Translation copyright© 1996, 2004, 2007 by Tyndale House Foundation. Used by permission of Tyndale House Publishers, Inc. Carol Stream, Illinois 60188. All rights reserved.

Scripture quotations marked MSG are taken from *THE MESSAGE*. Copyright © by Eugene H. Peterson, 1993, 1994, 1995, 1996, 2000, 2001, 2002. Used by permission of NavPress Publishing Group.

Published by Barbour Publishing, Inc., P.O. Box 719, Uhrichsville, Ohio 44683, www.barbourbooks.com

Our mission is to publish and distribute inspirational products offering exceptional value and biblical encouragement to the masses.

Member of the
Evangelical Christian
Publishers Association

Printed in the United States of America.

Open *the* Windows *of* *Heaven*

❧

Blessings for Women

❧

BARBOUR
PUBLISHING

Contents

Introduction

> *"He is the faithful God who keeps his covenant for a thousand generations and lavishes his unfailing love on those who love him and obey his commands."*
>
> DEUTERONOMY 7:9 NLT

Women are tenderhearted and compassionate, often carrying other women's burdens in an attempt to lighten another's load. With all the stress and worries to distract, it's easy to miss the blessings that God has poured out in our everyday lives. Like Elijah who did not find God's presence in the raging fire or billowing winds, God often reveals Himself in the whispers—a child's laughter, a glorious sunset, a life well lived. Don't be surprised if God meets you even in the darkness, but never without a hand to guide you. *Open the Widows of Heaven* will help train your ears for those whispers, wherever you are, and awaken your heart to the abundant treasure that already belongs to you in Christ.

More Than Blue Skies:
The Heavenlies

The heavens are telling of the
glory of God; and their expanse is
declaring the work of His hands.
PSALM 19:1 NASB

*A*bby waited impatiently for the red light to turn green, overwhelmed by troubles that burdened her life. Looking to heaven for inspiration, she noticed a glorious rainbow arching across the sky. Hoping to share the experience she glanced around for additional onlookers, but out of the masses of drivers, not one seemed to notice.

There is a great reminder of God's attributes painted across the horizon every single day. In those times when you start to feel overwhelmed and the worries of life overtake you, don't miss it. Instead, put down the dishes, turn off the TV, and go outside to watch the sky.

"Nature is fuel for the soul," says Richard Ryan, lead author and professor of psychology at the University of Rochester. "Often when we feel depleted we reach for a cup of coffee, but research suggests a better way to get energized is to connect with nature."

Gaze at the clouds going by, the birds soaring through the atmosphere. Feel the wind blowing through your hair. Look how great the sky and how much greater its Creator! The heavens are God's declaration that He is gloriously alive and beautifully masterful, in the heavens and on the earth. We are but tiny creatures beneath the glorious skies, and the One who maintains all this is surely big enough to have the circumstances of life under His control.

For ever since the world was created,
people have seen the earth and sky. Through
everything God made, they can clearly
see his invisible qualities—his eternal power
and divine nature. So they have no
excuse for not knowing God.
ROMANS 1:20 NLT

When I consider thy heavens, the work
of thy fingers, the moon and the stars,
which thou hast ordained; what is man,
that thou art mindful of him? and the
son of man, that thou visitest him?
PSALM 8:3–4 KJV

"Is not God in the height of heaven?
Look also at the distant stars,
how high they are!"
JOB 22:12 NASB

Never lose an opportunity of seeing
anything that is beautiful; for beauty is
God's handwriting—a wayside sacrament.
Welcome it in every fair face, in every fair sky,
in every fair flower, and thank God
for it as a cup of blessing.

RALPH WALDO EMERSON

The best remedy for those who are afraid,
lonely or unhappy is to go outside, somewhere
where they can be quiet, alone with the heavens,
nature and God. Because only then does
one feel that all is as it should be.

ANNE FRANK

[Jesus said,] "Walk out into the
fields and look at the wildflowers."
Matthew 6:28 msg

Our God cares about details. You see it
throughout His creation. Every species unique
and every creature unique within its species.
Human beings, created in His image and yet each
one of a kind. Flowers and trees awash with color
and refinement, even those growing along the
highway, sown as it were by the wind. When
you wonder if God is interested in the details
of your life, consider the evidence demonstrated
in nature. He cares about everything—
no matter how inconsequential.

Lift Up My Eyes

Lord, thank You for the lovely display of glory
in the heavens. Each brilliant sunrise and sunset
is a reminder not only of Your power but also of
Your artistry. Teach me to look up and beyond
the earthly circumstances around me, especially
on days when I feel hopeless and overwhelmed.
Your attributes are so easily seen if I will only take
a conscious moment to enjoy the vastness and
beauty of Your canvas, the sky.

*And also carefully guard yourselves so
that you don't look up into the skies and see
the sun and moon and stars, all the constellations
of the skies, and be seduced into worshiping
and serving them. God set them out for
everybody's benefit, everywhere.*

DEUTERONOMY 4:19 MSG

❧

*The LORD merely spoke,
and the heavens were created.*

PSALM 33:6 NLT

❧

*Look up into the heavens.
Who created all the stars?
He brings them out like an army,
one after another,
calling each by its name.
Because of his great power and
incomparable strength,
not a single one is missing.*

ISAIAH 40:26 NLT

Praise Him, sun and moon;
Praise Him, all stars of light!
Praise Him, highest heavens. . .
For He commanded and they were created.
He has also established them forever and ever;
He has made a decree which will not pass away.

PSALM 148:3–6 NASB

❧

Lift up your eyes to the heavens,
and look upon the earth beneath: for the
heavens shall vanish away like smoke,
and the earth shall wax old like a garment,
and they that dwell therein shall die in like
manner: but my salvation shall be for ever,
and my righteousness shall not be abolished.

ISAIAH 51:6 KJV

*Happy are those who hear
the joyful call to worship,
for they will walk in the
light of your presence, LORD.*
PSALM 89:15 NLT

Close your eyes and imagine yourself sitting on
the beach, a warm breeze tickling your skin and
the comforting sound of waves breaking on the
shore. Or think of yourself in a garden, the sounds
of songbirds and enchanting fragrances in every
direction. Place yourself anywhere, but know that
nothing can compare to being in the presence of
God. The treasures of the universe are stored there,
His love surrounds you, and peace flows like a
beautiful river. Come and enjoy.

Brilliant Reminders

Father, as I look into the night sky, each sparkle of
light is a glorious indication of Your faithfulness.
I can't help but feel small when I visualize the
vastness of Your universe. How insignificant I am
in light of how great You are, yet, You care for me,
enough to orchestrate even the smallest details
of my life. How blessed I am to know You,
the Creator of the heavens!

I love to think of nature as an unlimited
broadcasting station, through which God speaks
to us every hour, if we only will tune in.

GEORGE WASHINGTON CARVER

❧

Any one thing in the creation is
sufficient to demonstrate a Providence
to an humble and grateful mind.

EPICTETUS

❧

But who can paint like Nature?
Can imagination boast,
Amid its gay creation, hues like hers?

JAMES THOMSON

*A Match Made
in Heaven: Marriage*

Therefore a man leaves his father and mother and embraces his wife. They become one flesh.
GENESIS 2:24 MSG

Crystal married her high school sweetheart, but after about a dozen years of marriage, she wondered if she had missed out. What if she hadn't married her soul mate? What if there was that special someone still out there waiting for her?

There are periods in most marriages when a wife wonders if she married the right person. You might be going through a season right now in which the two of you are just not connecting and the same questions have crossed your mind—could life be better with someone else? Perhaps you've never really gotten along with your spouse, and it seems the relationship will always be distant. You wonder, "Is he my soul mate?"

It wasn't until a friend's husband died suddenly in a car accident that Crystal discovered a soul mate isn't someone you find; it's someone you become. It is possible to have a close flourishing relationship, but it takes intentional and prayerful work, which starts with you. There is almost always hope, even often despite complicated circumstances.

Your spouse is a gift, even in his imperfections. And with prayer and seeds of good works planted into your marriage, you will see springs of life come from a dehydrated relationship. Instead of looking for a soul mate, start asking yourself today what you need to do to become one.

"At last!" the man exclaimed. "This one is
bone from my bone, and flesh from my flesh!"
GENESIS 2:23 NLT

❧

A cord of three strands is not quickly torn apart.
ECCLESIASTES 4:12 NASB

❧

Because the LORD hath been witness between
thee and the wife of thy youth. . .yet is she thy
companion, and the wife of thy covenant.
MALACHI 2:14 KJV

Keep your eyes wide open before
marriage, half shut afterwards.
BENJAMIN FRANKLIN

There is no more lovely, friendly or
charming relationship, communion
or company, than a good marriage.
MARTIN LUTHER

Marriage is a thing you've got
to give your whole mind to.
HENRIK IBSEN

One must learn love and go through a
good deal of suffering to get to it. . .and the
journey is always towards the other soul.
D. H. LAWRENCE

Love each other with genuine affection,
and take delight in honoring each other.
ROMANS 12:10 NLT

Jesus' ultimate sacrifice—laying down His life so that all humanity could experience eternal life—showed true devotion. His willingness to go to the cross gave you the opportunity to experience an intimacy with God that was not available before. Likewise you can honor others with the same love. That strength and power of love resides within you. God gave you the ability to show His love to everyone you meet. Be bold! Be courageous! Love like Jesus does! It's in you!

Make Us One

God, forgive me when I forget my spouse is
Your gift. Prick my heart when I use words
that tear my husband down. Teach me, instead,
how to encourage him when he fails. I want my
marriage to honor You because our relationship
is a reflection of Your love toward Your people,
and even though we are both less than perfect,
through prayer, we can represent Your forgiveness
and unconditional acceptance to the world.

The two of them, the Man and his Wife,
were naked, but they felt no shame.
GENESIS 2:25 MSG

Honor marriage, and guard the sacredness
of sexual intimacy between wife and husband.
HEBREWS 13:4 MSG

For a husband is the head of his wife as Christ is the
head of the church. He is the Savior of his body, the
church. As the church submits to Christ, so you wives
should submit to your husbands in everything.
EPHESIANS 5:23–24 NLT

*Husbands, love your wives, even as Christ
also loved the church, and gave himself for it;
that he might sanctify and cleanse it with
the washing of water by the word, that he
might present it to himself a glorious church,
not having spot, or wrinkle, or any such thing;
but that it should be holy and without blemish.
So ought men to love their wives as their own
bodies. He that loveth his wife loveth himself.
For no man ever yet hated his own flesh;
but nourisheth and cherisheth it,
even as the Lord the church.*
EPHESIANS 5:25–29 KJV

The wise woman builds her house.
PROVERBS 14:1 NASB

The influence of a woman on her family is phenomenal—for good and for bad. Sadly, some women weaken their families through selfishness, ambition, and carelessness. The vigilant, wise, and godly woman holds her family together, makes sacrifices to ensure its stability, and entreats God's blessing with her prayers. You can be that kind of woman—the kind that builds up and strengthens. Ask God to help you. He will show you how.

―――― ❧ ――――

Mercy's Matrimony

Father, give me the grace and wisdom to know
how to be a blessing to my spouse, even when I
know he doesn't deserve it. And in the same way,
remind me to live humbly and admit my own
faults when I'm wrong. Through unconditional
love that only comes through You, knit our hearts
closer together and bless us with the kind of
marriage that brings forth fruit and honors You.

―――― ❧ ――――

There is no sorrow like a love denied
Nor any joy like love that has its will.

RICHARD HOVEY

※

He that hath wife and children hath given
hostages to fortune; for they are impediments
to great enterprises, either of virtue or mischief.

FRANCIS BACON

※

With grace the bride and bridegroom speed;
Thy love their pattern be;
May heart with heart be true indeed,
As knit, O Lord, in Thee.

JOHN BERRIDGE

Freedom from Perfection

And He has said to me, "My grace is sufficient for you, for power is perfected in weakness."
2 CORINTHIANS 12:9 NASB

*J*onathan had a learning disability and speech impediment, but that didn't deter his calling—evangelism. He kindly and intentionally approached strangers in public saying, "Sir, can I tell you about my Savior Jesus Christ? I'm not a perfect man, but one day I will be. . . ."

Have you ever felt totally incompetent for a task? Maybe you only volunteered to organize women's events in your church because no one else would. Perhaps you long to start an orphans' ministry but fear failure.

G. K. Chesterton once said, "A thing worth doing is worth doing badly." In other words, it's good to fulfill the desires of your heart, even when you feel insecure about the outcome. When you minister despite your inabilities, that's when God receives the greatest glory. You can take no credit for results that were undeniably supernatural.

When Gideon took 22,000 men to battle, God reduced the army to 300. He said, "The people who are with you are too many for Me to give Midian into their hands, for Israel would become boastful, saying, 'My own power has delivered me.'" (Judges 7:2 NASB).

Don't let your shortcomings keep you from fulfilling the calling that tugs on your heart. God has already empowered you to bring about His purposes. All you have to do is just accept that it won't be perfect—that's exactly what makes it perfect for Him.

That's why I take pleasure in my weaknesses,
and in the insults, hardships, persecutions,
and troubles that I suffer for Christ.
For when I am weak, then I am strong.
2 CORINTHIANS 12:10 NLT

❦

"Haven't I commanded you? Strength! Courage!
Don't be timid; don't get discouraged. GOD,
your God, is with you every step you take."
JOSHUA 1:9 MSG

❦

"For He has brought low those who dwell on high,
the unassailable city; He lays it low, He lays it
low to the ground, He casts it to the dust."
ISAIAH 26:5 NASB

Our peace and confidence are to be found not in our empirical holiness, not in our progress toward perfection, but in the alien righteousness of Jesus Christ that covers our sinfulness and alone makes us acceptable before a holy God.

DONALD BLOESCH

A man can no more take in a supply of grace for the future than he can eat enough for the next six months, or take sufficient air into his lungs at one time to sustain life for a week. We must draw upon God's boundless store of grace from day to day as we need it.

DWIGHT L. MOODY

God affirms us, making us a sure thing in Christ,
putting his Yes within us. By his Spirit he has
stamped us with his eternal pledge—a sure
beginning of what he is destined to complete.
2 CORINTHIANS 1:21–22 MSG

The last time you bought a house or a car or
applied for a loan, were you preapproved? Good
feeling, isn't it? In a real sense, you have been
preapproved for God's kingdom. He's given you
His Word and stamped you with His eternal
pledge. You belong to Him. He is fully committed
to helping you become all you were created to be.
You can turn your back on Him—it's true.
But He will never turn His back on you.

Call for Courage

Father, show me the callings I'm avoiding
because of a fear of failure. Help me to have the
discernment to discover what they are and the
courage to begin. Give me peace to accept my
own weaknesses and find the strength I need
through Your Holy Spirit. With You, all things are
possible. Give me faith to see beyond my own
abilities and envision the many possible ways
You can use me despite my shortcomings.

*Not that we are adequate in ourselves to
consider anything as coming from ourselves,
but our adequacy is from God.*
2 Corinthians 3:5 nasb

※

*"But as for you, be strong and courageous,
for your work will be rewarded."*
2 Chronicles 15:7 nlt

※

*But when they deliver you up, take no thought
how or what ye shall speak: for it shall be given
you in that same hour what ye shall speak.*
Matthew 10:19 kjv

But Moses pleaded with the LORD, "O Lord, I'm not very good with words. I never have been, and I'm not now, even though you have spoken to me. I get tongue-tied, and my words get tangled." Then the LORD asked Moses, "Who makes a person's mouth? Who decides whether people speak or do not speak, hear or do not hear, see or do not see? Is it not I, the LORD? Now go! I will be with you as you speak, and I will instruct you in what to say."

EXODUS 4:10–12 NLT

I can do all things through
Christ which strengtheneth me.
PHILIPPIANS 4:13 KJV

You're probably busier than you've ever been—
doing more than you've ever done. Maybe
you feel exhausted—physically, mentally, and
emotionally. God has given you strength for your
days—even the toughest ones. He is the source
you can draw on when you feel your supply is
running low. You don't have to go at life alone.
When you reach for Him, He's always there,
ready to refresh you. Find quiet moments to
dip your soul into His supply. You'll come
away strengthened and renewed.

Supernatural Strength

God, there are moments when I feel like I
just can't work in ministry any longer, but I
know my strength comes only from You.
Help me find the time to replenish myself by
reading Your Word and seeking Your heart
through prayer. I know I can't do anything on
my own, so forgive me for the times I neglect
to open my heart and receive from You.

The Christian ideal, it is said, has not been tried and found wanting; it has been found difficult and left untried.

G. K. CHESTERTON

❧

The most secret, sacred wish that lies deep down at the bottom of your heart, the wonderful thing that you hardly dare to look at. . .because it seems too far beyond anything that you are. . .that is just the very thing that God is wishing you to do or be for him. And. . .the dawning of that secret dream was the Voice of God himself telling you to arise and come up higher because he had need of you.

EMMET FOX

Encouragement
from Above

Kind words are like honey—
sweet to the soul and healthy for the body.
PROVERBS 16:24 NLT

———— ❧ ————

Samuel Hopkins, a minister in the Second Great Awakening, once experienced a "Christ-less, graceless state" when he received encouragement from a fellow minister's wife. "She told me that she had [prayed] respecting me. . .[and] that she trusted I should receive light and comfort and doubted not that He intended yet to do great things by me."

Hopkins never forgot her simple reassurance and went on to inspire others like William Ellery Channing who influenced Emerson and Thoreau and battled slavery.

Sometimes in order to navigate the stale waters of self-pity we need a strong wind of inspiration. When those reinforcements come, don't dismiss them with replies of self-described faults, such as, "I'm really not that good" or "I'm just lucky." These responses may seem humble, but they are more closely related to ungratefulness.

Rather, write down those words and meditate on how they inspire you. Let them sink into your soul like a soothing balm, especially in times of uncertainty and pain.

When Saul of Tarsus, a persecutor of Christians, approached the apostles as a convert, everyone but Barnabas was afraid to trust him. The man known as the "son of encouragement" took the man who became the Apostle Paul, into his fellowship, and the rest is New Testament history.

Do you receive encouragement from fellow Christians or reject it? Look for the Barnabases God has sent to strengthen your heart and treasure each word as a gift.

The tongue can bring death or life;
those who love to talk will reap the consequences.
PROVERBS 18:21 NLT

❧

Watch the way you talk. Let nothing
foul or dirty come out of your mouth.
Say only what helps, each word a gift.
EPHESIANS 4:29 MSG

❧

Faithful are the wounds of a friend;
but the kisses of an enemy are deceitful.
PROVERBS 27:6 KJV

❧

The speech of a good person
is worth waiting for.
PROVERBS 10:20 MSG

His words were simple words enough
And yet he used them so
That what in other mouths was rough
In his seemed musical and low.

JAMES RUSSELL LOWELL

No man is the whole of himself;
his friends are the rest of him.

HARRY EMERSON FOSDICK

But words are things, and a small drop of ink,
Falling like dew upon a thought, produces
That which makes thousands,
perhaps millions, think.

LORD BYRON

Think of ways to motivate one another
to acts of love and good works.
HEBREWS 10:24 NLT

The great thing about Christian community is
that we inspire each other in this Christian walk.
Haven't you caught someone red-handed in
some kind of faithful act, and felt inspired? And
who knows how many times your faith has been
spotted and someone made a better choice "next
time" because they saw the choice you made.
That's the wonder of rubbing elbows in the
fray together. Faith alone strengthens you.
But faith together inspires more faith!

Grace to Receive

Lord, I am thankful for those Christians You
have put into my life to bring words of healing
and encouragement. Help me to accept their
kindness with grace and gratitude and not ignore
the words that were sent for my good. Help me
press them into my heart and find inspiration
to do greater things for Your kingdom,
even in the midst of my own insecurities.

*"How beautiful are the feet of
messengers who bring good news!"*
ROMANS 10:15 NLT

❧

*A word out of your mouth may seem
of no account, but it can accomplish
nearly anything—or destroy it!*
JAMES 3:5 MSG

❧

The words of a wise man's mouth are gracious.
ECCLESIASTES 10:12 KJV

❧

A word spoken in due season, how good is it!
PROVERBS 15:23 KJV

Each of us is to please his neighbor
for his good, to his edification.
ROMANS 15:2 NASB

So encourage each other and build each
other up, just as you are already doing.
1 THESSALONIANS 5:11 NLT

Refuse good advice and watch your plans fail;
take good counsel and watch them succeed.
PROVERBS 15:22 MSG

Worry weighs a person down;
an encouraging word cheers a person up.
PROVERBS 12:25 NLT

[God] is gracious to the humble.
PROVERBS 3:34 NLT

For many people, it's difficult to receive what they don't feel they have earned. Whether it's a sense of independence or pride, such an attitude will rob you of the best this life has to offer. You must be able to receive God's love, even when you don't feel lovable, and God's goodness, even when you don't feel deserving. God has freely given you everything—His kingdom! Don't stand on the sidelines whispering, "I'm not worthy." Humble yourself and receive.

Giving It Away

God, as I learn to identify the Barnabases in my life, teach me to be a "son of encouragement" to others in my sphere of influence. Just as I have been uplifted by my sisters and brothers in Christ, show me those who need words of grace and re-assurance. Small as they are, kind expressions are often hard to give away. Give me confidence and wisdom to know when and what to say.

Friendship is precious, not only in the shade,
but in the sunshine of life.

THOMAS JEFFERSON

❧

It is not for minds like ours to give or to receive
flattery; yet the praises of sincerity have ever
been permitted to the voice of friendship.

LORD BYRON

❧

Words are the physicians of a mind diseased.

AESCHYLUS

❧

Our chief want is someone who will inspire
us to be what we know we could be.

RALPH WALDO EMERSON

The Perfect Parent:
God's Love

*And [Jesus] took [the children] in His arms and
began blessing them, laying His hands on them.*
MARK 10:16 NASB

❦

*J*anet was a young mom who lost her husband
in a tragic car accident. She often prayed for her
two small children, fearful of what psychological
damage they would sustain growing up without
a father. But each time she desperately prayed for
them, God would assure her, "You have nothing
to fear; *I* am their Father."

"I knew God was telling me He loved them
more than I did," Janet said. "And He can better
care for them than any earthly father." Being
a parent is a daunting task. There are so many
responsibilities. And modern psychologists are
sometimes not kind to parents, often blaming
them for the troubles of each generation. If only
children came with an instruction manual the day
they were born!

You can breathe easy, however, knowing you are not the perfect parent. You will make mistakes that hurt. And you can't shelter them from life which may cause lasting scars at times.

But do not be afraid—God is perfect, and He is their heavenly Father. They are safe in His care. Jesus declared their importance to God saying, "I say to you that [the children's] angels in heaven continually see the face of My Father who is in heaven" (Matthew 18:10 NASB). God is offering every parent peace of mind when you trust the future of your children into His ever-loving care.

*And [they] said to Him, "Do You hear what
these children are saying?" And Jesus said to
them, "Yes; have you never read, 'Out of the
mouth of infants and nursing babies You
have prepared praise for Yourself'?"*
MATTHEW 21:16 NASB

❧

*You have taught children and infants
to tell of your strength, silencing your
enemies and all who oppose you.*
PSALM 8:2 NLT

❧

*Don't you see that children are God's best gift?
the fruit of the womb his generous legacy?
Like a warrior's fistful of arrows are the
children of a vigorous youth.*
PSALM 127:3–4 MSG

Build me a son, O Lord, who will be strong
enough to know when he is weak, and brave
enough to face himself when he is afraid; one
who will be proud and unbending in honest
defeat, and humble and gentle in victory.

DOUGLAS MACARTHUR

And first, I give to good fathers and mothers,
but in trust for their children, nevertheless,
all good little words of praise and all quaint
pet names, and I charge said parents to use
them justly, but generously, as the needs
of their children shall require.

THE HOBO'S WILL, WILLISTON FISH

All thy children shall be taught of the LORD;
and great shall be the peace of thy children.
ISAIAH 54:13 KJV

There's no heritage like the knowledge of God's
love. There's no inheritance as empowering.
As you live your life of faith before your family,
it's like stocking a vault that will bless everyone.
And it's never too late to begin. As you live
authentically before God, you leave a blueprint
for those who are watching. That example can
last for generations, beyond your view, more
influential than you can fathom.

Precious Possessions

Dear Father, I know You love and care for my children even more than I do. Help me to live in peace, knowing they are in Your hands. No matter what happens, I can trust You. Remind me that I have no reason to worry about their future when I walk in faith because You will never leave or forsake Your people. Thank You for sending Your angels to watch over each and every child.

"If a man has a hundred sheep and one of them wanders away, what will he do? Won't he leave the ninety-nine others on the hills and go out to search for the one that is lost? And if he finds it, I tell you the truth, he will rejoice over it more than over the ninety-nine that didn't wander away! In the same way, it is not my heavenly Father's will that even one of these little ones should perish."

MATTHEW 18:12–14 NLT

*But Jesus called for them, saying, "Permit the
children to come to Me, and do not hinder them,
for the kingdom of God belongs to such as these."*
Luke 18:16 nasb

❧

*Father to the fatherless, defender of widows—
this is God, whose dwelling is holy.
God places the lonely in families;
he sets the prisoners free and gives them joy.*
Psalm 68:5–6 nlt

❧

*"And I will be a father to you,
and you shall be sons and daughters
to Me," says the Lord Almighty.*
2 Corinthians 6:18 nasb

*But if any of you lacks wisdom, let him
ask of God, who gives to all generously and
without reproach, and it will be given to him.*
JAMES 1:5 NASB

You can read books and ask others for advice
as you raise your children, but how can you be
assured what you're doing is the best for them?
Just as your children come to you with questions,
take your questions to God, your heavenly Father.
No question is too small or too big. You can't
stump Him, because He knows you and your
children intimately. After all, He has created you
all. God is the best resource you can find.

Lessons Learned

Lord, I feel so guilty each time I mess up and
say or do something to my children that I know
was selfish or too harsh. I pray that You would
give me wisdom and teach me how to avoid
situations like that in the future. In the meantime,
show me how to use this mistake to teach my
children how to apologize and forgive,
as You have forgiven me today.

It is a wise father that knows his own child.

WILLIAM SHAKESPEARE

❧

With filial confidence inspired,
Can lift to Heaven an unpresumptuous eye,
And smiling say, My Father made them all!

WILLIAM COWPER

❧

Parents must not be cruel ostriches,
and expose their young ones to harm and
danger; nor yet must they be such fond apes,
who are said to hug their cubs so closely
that they kill them with their embraces.

THOMAS LYE

The Gift of Purpose

God will make this happen,
for he who calls you is faithful.
1 Thessalonians 5:24 nlt

––––––––– ❧ –––––––––

*H*ave you lost your life's dreams? Did you once have passions that have been trampled by the fast pace of everyday living? Do you feel like you've lost your direction and drive?

Every Christian has a calling in life. We all possess gifts to fulfill a specific role, a purpose, which God has established in the kingdom. Not one believer is unimportant to God's plan. But you may feel forgotten or inhibited by necessary responsibilities—providing for a family, caring for children, attending aging parents. You may wonder, *Where is the fulfillment of God's calling in my life?*

God has not forgotten His purpose for you. The works He began in you will not go unfulfilled. At the right time, God will awaken the seeds that were planted for His intentions and in due time they will produce fruit.

Abram and Sarai were promised descendants that would number the stars in the sky, but at eighty-five years old the couple was still childless. Imagine their disappointment! It wasn't until Sarai reached ninety that God decided it was time to keep His word. He waited until there would be no doubt where this miracle child came from.

God will bring about the fruition of His promises in your life as well. In the meantime, wait on the Lord, pray, and hold on to the hope that the One who called you will bring about your purpose in His time.

After you have suffered for a little while,
the God of all grace, who called you to His
eternal glory in Christ, will Himself perfect,
confirm, strengthen and establish you.
1 PETER 5:10 NASB

And I am certain that God, who began
the good work within you, will continue
his work until it is finally finished on
the day when Christ Jesus returns.
PHILIPPIANS 1:6 NLT

To every thing there is a season,
and a time to every purpose under the heaven.
ECCLESIASTES 3:1 KJV

Strength in Waiting

God, it doesn't seem too long ago when I had plans to do great things for You. I know You have called me for Your purpose, but I feel lost. Help me to have the faith that You will fulfill those dreams despite the many circumstances in this life that seem to get in the way. I pray for the strength to wait and the patience to see what You have already planned to do.

*Yet God has made everything beautiful for its own
time. He has planted eternity in the human heart,
but even so, people cannot see the whole scope of
God's work from beginning to end.*
ECCLESIASTES 3:11 NLT

*And we know that God causes all things to work
together for good to those who love God, to those
who are called according to His purpose.*
ROMANS 8:28 NASB

*Wait on the LORD: be of good courage, and he shall
strengthen thine heart: wait, I say, on the LORD.*
PSALM 27:14 KJV

As a well-spent day brings happy sleep,
so life well used brings happy death.

Leonardo Da Vinci

❧

Hope springs eternal in the human breast:
Man never is, but always to be blest.
The soul, uneasy and confined from home,
Rests and expatiates in a life to come.

Alexander Pope

❧

Yet I doubt not through the ages
one increasing purpose runs,
And the thoughts of men are widened
with the process of the suns.

Tennyson

❧

Patience is the best remedy for every trouble.

Plautus

Commit your works to the Lord
and your plans will be established.
PROVERBS 16:3 NASB

Whatever God has called you to accomplish in
your life, He has not called you to accomplish
alone. He is always there, providing you with
the resources you need to get the job done. That
doesn't mean you won't stumble along the way
or encounter difficulties. But it does mean that
you can call upon the counsel and resources of
almighty God to help you. Whether you need
wisdom, inspiration, confidence, strength, or just
plain tenacity, you will find your answer in Him.

Little Victories

Lord, as I wait for You to fulfill Your work in my life, show me the blessings that I may be missing. I know this is just a season that I must work through, but I don't want to overlook the little victories that take place all around me. I know You work all things together for the good of Your people. How is today working for Your good in me?

"But he knows where I am going. And when
he tests me, I will come out as pure as gold."
JOB 23:10 NLT

⁊⁊

But they that wait upon the LORD shall renew
their strength; they shall mount up with wings
as eagles; they shall run, and not be weary;
and they shall walk, and not faint.
ISAIAH 40:31 KJV

⁊⁊

God, the one and only—I'll wait as long as he says.
Everything I hope for comes from him.
PSALM 62:5 MSG

He that can have Patience,
can have what he will.

<small>BENJAMIN FRANKLIN</small>

❧

Endurance is the crowning quality,
and patience all the passion of great hearts.

<small>JAMES RUSSELL LOWELL</small>

❧

Though the mills of God grind slowly, yet they
grind exceeding small; Though with patience He
stands waiting, with exactness grinds He all.

<small>FRIEDRICH</small>

❧

The key to everything is patience. You get the
chicken by hatching the egg, not by smashing it.

<small>ARNOLD GLASOW</small>

Rest in the LORD, and wait patiently for him.
PSALM 37:7 KJV

Do you remember as a child waiting for Christmas morning or to open your presents on your birthday? "Just wait. It will all happen in due time," your mother would say. God won't withhold from you just to be cruel or make a point, but He does see the big picture, and He knows the right when, where, and how. So don't get anxious, just wait. You will see what God has promised you—all in due time.

Strength for Today

Father, some days I am encouraged and confident, but today I need extra strength to wait for Your will. The burdens of life are difficult to bear, but You promise through Your Word that I can trust You to shoulder those heavy loads. I don't have to go through these things alone. When I'm worried and stressed and circumstances feel beyond my control, remind me to cast my cares on You.

No great work is ever done in a hurry. To develop
a great scientific discovery, to paint a great picture,
to write an immortal poem, to become a minister,
or a famous general—to do anything great
requires time, patience, and perseverance.

W. J. Wilmont Buxton

A life without a purpose is a languid,
drifting thing. Every day we ought to
renew our purpose, saying to ourselves:
This day let us make a sound beginning,
for what we have hitherto done is nought.

Thomas à Kempis

'Tis a Gift to Be Simple

But God has chosen the foolish things of
the world to shame the wise, and God
has chosen the weak things of the world
to shame the things which are strong.

1 Corinthians 1:27 nasb

Mary of Nazareth was a young woman of humble means. She was surprised and confused when the angel Gabriel explained she was chosen by God to be the mother of His Son. She later declared, "[God] has had regard for the humble state of His bondslave. . .[He] has exalted those who were humble" (Luke 1:48, 52 nasb).

Sometimes a great life is a simple one. Mary never traveled the world or wrote a book or attained great wealth. She lived a meek life that honored Jehovah, and that alone made her the perfect candidate to be "blessed among women" and the one who was favored by God!

In a society that idolizes experiences—the finest destinations, exotic foods, thrilling adventures—it's tempting to believe that a simple life is an unsuccessful one. But there are riches far more valuable than luxury in a life well-pleasing to God, no matter how modest. Elizabeth Elliot wrote, "We accept and thank God for what is given, not allowing the 'not given' to spoil it."

Perhaps your day consists of housework and child rearing. Maybe you've watched with envy while others live extravagantly. Just know that God sees the faithfulness of a simple life that is lived for His glory, and He will reward you in due time.

*The meek also shall increase their joy in
the L*ORD*, and the poor among men
shall rejoice in the Holy One of Israel.*
ISAIAH 29:19 KJV

*Listen, dear friends. Isn't it clear by now that
God operates quite differently? He chose the
world's down-and-out as the kingdom's first
citizens, with full rights and privileges.*
JAMES 2:5 MSG

*Our hearts ache, but we always have joy.
We are poor, but we give spiritual riches to others.
We own nothing, and yet we have everything.*
2 CORINTHIANS 6:10 NLT

New Perspective

Lord, there are times when I'm tempted to
envy my friends who have more than I do.
I see their nice clothes and expensive vacations,
and I forget how truly blessed I am. Even though
I know life isn't measured by wealth, it often
seems like everyone else has found happiness
and fulfillment while I sit by and watch.
Will You help me find contentment and
joy within the life I've been given?

The meek will he guide in judgment:
and the meek will he teach his way.
PSALM 25:9 KJV

For they say, "[Paul's] letters are weighty
and strong, but his personal presence is
unimpressive and his speech contemptible."
2 CORINTHIANS 10:10 NASB

"You're blessed when you're content with just
who you are—no more, no less. That's the
moment you find yourselves proud owners
of everything that can't be bought."
MATTHEW 5:5 MSG

No race can prosper until it learns
that there is as much dignity in tilling
the field as in writing a poem.
BOOKER T. WASHINGTON

The Magi were taught by the heavens to
follow a star; and it brought them, not to
a paralyzing disclosure of the Transcendent,
but to a little boy on his mother's knee.
EVELYN UNDERHILL

The world is moved along, not only by the mighty
shoves of its heroes, but also by the aggregate of
the tiny pushes of each honest worker.
HELEN KELLER

With humility comes wisdom.
PROVERBS 11:2 NLT

The Bible says that Jesus is the only begotten
Son of God, ruling and reigning with His Father
from Their heavenly throne room. And yet, He
did the unthinkable. He chose to be born as a
baby, live as one of us, and then suffer reproach
and abuse, finally death. He humbled Himself
and allowed Himself to be placed on the cross—
for you. His humility accomplished the plan of
salvation. Imagine what your humble obedience
to His will can accomplish.

Lasting Pleasures

Father, I'm so easily distracted by the priorities of this world—money, selfish ambition, thrill of adventure. But these things don't last. There is so much more to life than temporary pleasures. I want to focus on the joys in life that won't fade away. Teach me to cultivate the seeds of Your spirit in me and my household so that we might experience fruit that will always satisfy.

*Don't be selfish; don't try to impress others.
Be humble, thinking of others as
better than yourselves.*
PHILIPPIANS 2:3 NLT

❦

*The brother of humble circumstances
is to glory in his high position.*
JAMES 1:9 NASB

❦

*I [Paul] have learned to be content in whatever
circumstances I am. I know how to get along with
humble means, and I also know how to live in
prosperity; in any and every circumstance I have
learned the secret of being filled and going hungry,
both of having abundance and suffering need.*
PHILIPPIANS 4:11–12 NASB

Little drops of water, little grains of sand,
Make the mighty ocean and the pleasant land.
So the little minutes, humble though they be,
Make the mighty ages of eternity.

JULIA A. FLETCHER CARNEY

❧

'Tis better to be lowly born,
And range with humble livers in content,
Than to be perked up in a glistering grief,
And wear a golden sorrow.

WILLIAM SHAKESPEARE

❧

Meek and lowly, pure and holy,
Chief among the "blessed three."

CHARLES JEFFERYS

Seek those things which are above, where Christ sitteth on the right hand of God. Set your affection on things above, not on things on the earth.
COLOSSIANS 3:1–2 KJV

Human beings can be hopelessly shortsighted. But the person who sees past today and plans for eternity has both the present and the future in mind. When you accepted Christ's sacrifice for you on the cross and asked God to forgive your sins, your future in heaven was sealed. But the Bible also talks about laying up treasure in heaven. Place your priorities on those things that are eternal rather than those things that are just for this world alone.

All I Possess

Contentment is a rare gift in our society,
which is filled with people who always thirst
for more than they have. Teach me to be satisfied
no matter in what circumstances I find myself.
I realize that there will always be those who have
more than me in both possessions and talents,
but all I own, which isn't much, I give to You
for the service of Your kingdom.

God, grant me the serenity to accept
the things I cannot change;
Courage to change the things I can;
And the wisdom to know the difference.
Living one day at a time;
Enjoying one moment at a time.
Accepting hardship as the pathway to peace;
Taking, as He did, this sinful world
as it is, not as I would have it;
Trusting that He will make all things right,
If I surrender to His will;
That I may be reasonably happy in this life,
And supremely happy with
Him forever in the next.
Amen.

REINHOLD NIEBUHR, THE SERENITY PRAYER

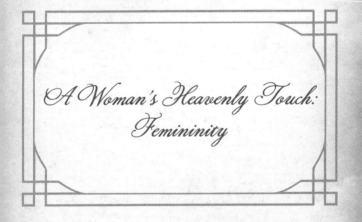

A Woman's Heavenly Touch:
Femininity

God created man in His own image,
in the image of God He created him;
male and female He created them.

GENESIS 1:27 NASB

*F*or generations, society has struggled with the role of femininity. Many have tried to blur the differences between man and woman, attempting to make everyone the same, but it's necessary to preserve our uniquenesses. It takes both to complete the perfect picture of creation.

Without the feminine to balance the masculine, the reflection of God's image is unfinished both spiritually and relationally. Both man and woman were created in the image of God, not simply man alone.

Scripture often describes God in word pictures that transcend gender, but for our human understanding, some of the metaphors that describe God are uniquely feminine: a comforting mother

(Isaiah 66:12–13), a nursing caretaker (Numbers 11:12), one who births and protects (Isaiah 46:3–4). Man and woman are as equal and different as the Trinity itself. Even though God refers to Himself in masculine terms, His character reflects both. As a woman, you can beautifully echo God's image in ways a man cannot and vice versa.

Embrace your femininity and display it with confidence, glorifying the One who gifted it to you. Dress beautifully, but modestly, because your body belongs to God. Speak words that heal, not bleed, because your speech overflows from the heart, a residence of the Holy Spirit. Seek to be nurturing, soft, and supportive, displaying unconditional love. Proudly embrace the role God has entrusted to you, reflecting those nurturing parts of the character of God that are most precisely seen through the daughters of Eve.

Charm can mislead and beauty soon fades.
The woman to be admired and praised is
the woman who lives in the Fear-of-God.
PROVERBS 31:30 MSG

❧

"For he took notice of his lowly servant girl, and
from now on all generations will call me blessed."
LUKE 1:48 NLT

❧

[A good woman] is clothed with strength and
dignity, and she laughs without fear of the future.
PROVERBS 31:25 NLT

Dual Reflection

Thank You, Father, for commending me as Your image bearer. Help me display the characteristics of femininity in Your honor and prick my heart if ever I am tempted to distort that image. Help me to respect both masculine and feminine in their respective roles and never degrade one below another. Make me aware of how my feminine qualities display Your character to the world around me and let me never forget how important they are.

And the king loved Esther more than any of the other young women. He was so delighted with her that he set the royal crown on her head and declared her queen instead of Vashti.
ESTHER 2:17 NLT

❧

Who can find a virtuous woman?
for her price is far above rubies.
PROVERBS 31:10 KJV

❧

Be good wives to your husbands, responsive to their needs. There are husbands who, indifferent as they are to any words about God, will be captivated by your life of holy beauty.
1 PETER 3:1–2 MSG

O woman! lovely woman! Nature made thee
To temper man: we had been brutes without you.
Angels are painted fair, to look like you:
There's in you all that we believe of heaven—
Amazing brightness, purity, and truth,
Eternal joy, and everlasting love.

THOMAS OTWAY

God's rarest blessing is,
after all, a good woman.

GEORGE MEREDITH

A good woman is a wondrous creature,
cleaving to the right and to the good under
all change: lovely in youthful comeliness,
lovely all her life long in comeliness of heart.

TENNYSON

"The LORD doesn't see things the way you see them. People judge by outward appearance, but the LORD looks at the heart."
1 SAMUEL 16:7 NLT

When God looks at you, He sees a beautiful woman, a temple worthy of His Spirit. He sees your virtuous life and your godly attitudes. He sees a person whose heart has been washed clean and fully submitted to His will and purpose. He sees a beauty that is often missed by others. He sees an inner beauty that transcends any physical characteristics—good or bad. God sees you as you really are.

Leaving a Legacy

Dear Lord, I realize that my femininity was created to glorify You and display parts of Your character to the world. But with those responsibilities comes great influence that if used poorly can also tear others down. Teach me to use my speech and emotions to encourage, nurture the hurting, and direct those in my guidance to walk closer with You, leaving a godly legacy behind me.

The man who finds a wife finds a treasure,
and he receives favor from the LORD.
PROVERBS 18:22 NLT

❧

"Now, my daughter, do not fear. I will do for you
whatever you ask, for all my people in the city
know that you are a woman of excellence."
RUTH 3:11 NASB

❧

"Can a mother forget her nursing child?
Can she feel no love for the child she has borne?
But even if that were possible,
I would not forget you!"
ISAIAH 49:15 NLT

Let a woman never be persuaded to forget
that her calling is not the lower and more
earthly one of self-assertion, but the higher
and more divine calling of self-sacrifice.

CHARLES KINGSLEY

❧

A witty woman is a treasure;
witty beauty is a power.

GEORGE MEREDITH

❧

Let no man value at a little price
A virtuous woman's counsel; her wing'd spirit
Is feather'd oftentimes with heavenly words.

GEORGE CHAPMAN

❧

What will not woman, gentle woman dare,
When strong affection stirs her spirit up?

ROBERT SOUTHEY

But we proved to be gentle among you, as a
nursing mother tenderly cares for her own children.
1 Thessalonians 2:7 nasb

❧

The Man, known as Adam, named his wife Eve
because she was the mother of all the living.
Genesis 3:20 msg

❧

He gives the childless woman a family,
making her a happy mother.
Psalm 113:9 nlt

❧

A gracious woman retaineth honour.
Proverbs 11:16 kjv

God's Love Letter:
The Word

How sweet are thy words unto my taste!
yea, sweeter than honey to my mouth!
Psalm 119:103 kjv

If you were separated from the man that you loved, would you not treasure every word of the letters he wrote? That's how every Christian should feel about the Bible. These are words straight from the heart of God; and while you are on this earth, separated from His physical presence, you can treasure His message—the greatest sonnet of love in history.

Not only is this love letter from God filled with passionate affection, deep comfort, and aged wisdom, it also provides training so you will know how to protect yourself from the weapons of the devil and the temptations of the heart that seek to destroy your relationship with Christ.

Scripture describes Jesus as "the word made flesh," meaning He was the embodiment of every principle, teaching, and moral law perfectly kept. When you study the Bible, you are exploring the very character of Christ Himself, an act of adoration and worship.

God's letter to His people is overflowing with stories of grace and forgiveness and love. It is more lovely and expressive than the writings of Shakespeare. The imagery and symbolism of biblical communication would put Wordsworth to shame. Each and every character in the scriptures was meant to communicate one idea to you—"This is how much I love you." Meditate and memorize every word, not because you have to, but because it is beautiful.

Jesus said to the people who believed in him,
"You are truly my disciples if you remain
faithful to my teachings. And you will know
the truth, and the truth will set you free."
JOHN 8:31–32 NLT

❧

For the word of God is living and active and
sharper than any two-edged sword, and piercing
as far as the division of soul and spirit, of both
joints and marrow, and able to judge the
thoughts and intentions of the heart.
HEBREWS 4:12 NASB

❧

Heaven and earth shall pass away,
but my words shall not pass away.
MATTHEW 24:35 KJV

Let your religion be less of a
theory and more of a love affair.

G. K. CHESTERTON

❧

The kingdom of God does not consist in talk, but
in power, that is, in works and practice. God loves
the "doers of the word" in faith and love, and
not the "mere hearers," who, like parrots, have
learned to utter certain expressions with readiness.

MARTIN LUTHER

❧

Do not have your concert first, and then tune
your instrument afterwards. Begin the day
with the Word of God and prayer, and get
first of all into harmony with Him.

HUDSON TAYLOR

Thy word is a lamp unto my feet,
and a light unto my path.
PSALM 119:105 KJV

If only life came with an instruction manual,
you've said to yourself. The Bible is filled with
stories of ordinary people who lived through
struggles and triumphs, heartache and joy.
Unlike the stories we see today on television,
not every story has a happy ending. People saw
consequences of their erroneous actions. Through
it all, God shines a light for our paths today.

Washing of the Word

Lord, my spirit overflows with gratitude to read the words of Your heart. I pray that each time I open the pages of the Bible the sense of Your love washes over me, filling me with the fruits of Your Spirit. Let each principle and proverb penetrate my soul and make me more like You so I can reflect the same love to others and minister Your wisdom to all who need it.

The teaching of your word gives light,
so even the simple can understand.
PSALM 119:130 NLT

❧

So will My word be which goes forth from My
mouth; it will not return to Me empty, without
accomplishing what I desire, and without
succeeding in the matter for which I sent it.
ISAIAH 55:11 NASB

❧

When you received his message from us,
you didn't think of our words as mere human
ideas. You accepted what we said as the very
word of God—which, of course, it is. And this
word continues to work in you who believe.
1 THESSALONIANS 2:13 NLT

Being born again, not of corruptible seed,
but of incorruptible, by the word of God,
which liveth and abideth for ever.
1 PETER 1:23 KJV

❧

Put on salvation as your helmet, and take the
sword of the Spirit, which is the word of God.
EPHESIANS 6:17 NLT

❧

But he answered and said, It is written,
Man shall not live by bread alone, but by every
word that proceedeth out of the mouth of God.
MATTHEW 4:4 KJV

Put on the full armor of God, so that you will be able to stand firm against the schemes of the devil.
EPHESIANS 6:11 NASB

It's a good idea for every woman to take a basic class in self-defense in order to protect herself in this predator-filled world. A wise woman will learn how to defend herself spiritually as well. God has provided you with a full suit of armor for that purpose—truth, righteousness, peace, faith, and salvation. Wear them everywhere you go. You do have an enemy, and he wants to take all you have. Be prepared to resist and defeat him.

A Powerful Weapon

Father, thank You for Your Word, which not only comforts me in times of distress, but also wields as a sword, helping me fight the spiritual battles of my life. I can open the pages of scripture and arm myself with truth and encouragement when temptations and trials taunt me. What a blessing to fill my heart with Your words that give me the strength to overcome anything that I face.

*My dear child, don't shrug off God's
discipline, but don't be crushed by it either.
It's the child he loves that he disciplines;
the child he embraces, he also corrects.*
HEBREWS 12:5–6 MSG

❦

*"I will put My law within them and on
their heart I will write it; and I will be
their God, and they shall be My people."*
JEREMIAH 31:33 NASB

❦

*The law of his God is in his heart;
His steps do not slip.*
PSALM 37:31 NASB

The Bible is a book of faith, and a book of doctrine, and a book of morals, and a book of religion, of especial revelation from God.

DANIEL WEBSTER

❧

The English Bible—a book which if everything else in our language should perish, would alone suffice to show the whole extent of its beauty and power.

LORD MACAULAY

❧

Time can take nothing from the Bible. It is the living monitor. Like the sun, it is the same in its light and influence to man this day which it was years ago. It can meet every present inquiry and console every present loss.

RICHARD CECIL

*"I take joy in doing your will, my God,
for your instructions are written on my heart."*
PSALM 40:8 NLT

❦

*"Listen to Me, you who know righteousness,
a people in whose heart is My law;
do not fear the reproach of man,
nor be dismayed at their revilings."*
ISAIAH 51:7 NASB

❦

*All scripture is given by inspiration of God,
and is profitable for doctrine, for reproof,
for correction, for instruction in righteousness.*
2 TIMOTHY 3:16 KJV

The Gift of Laughter

> *"Blessed are you who weep now,*
> *for you shall laugh."*
> LUKE 6:21 NASB

---

*L*aughter is powerful. Studies show it can lower blood pressure, ease stress, and help the circulatory system, as well as benefit people psychologically. Preschool children may laugh as often as 400 times a day, evidence of their carefree attitudes.

But life doesn't always give us reason to laugh. In our world, suffering is inevitable—tragedy happens, no matter how many good works or precautions are exercised. Christy couldn't stop a heart attack from taking her husband's life in his sleep. Baby Zena couldn't prevent her mother from physically abusing her. The Apostle Paul was blameless when the Romans kept him under house arrest, awaiting his execution. But from death row, he penned these words, "Rejoice in the Lord always; again I will say, rejoice!" (Phillipians 4:4 NASB).

How is your heart? Is it carefree and easy? Or is it weighed down with worry? The good news is that no matter what circumstances you're facing, a Christian can choose to live in joy, even if it is by faith alone. God's Word promises that He will take your burdens from you. Cast them onto His shoulders and live light.

Embrace your heavenly gift of joy, even when troubles find their way to your doorstep. Take a deep breath and dwell on the blessings you do have. Let your mind wander to pleasant memories and don't forget what God has promised. Go ahead—despite everything, throw back your head and laugh.

For the despondent, every day brings trouble;
for the happy heart, life is a continual feast.
PROVERBS 15:15 NLT

❧

Rejoice in the Lord always;
again I will say, rejoice!
PHILIPPIANS 4:4 NASB

❧

He continued, "Go home and prepare a feast,
holiday food and drink; and share it with those
who don't have anything: This day is holy to God.
Don't feel bad. The joy of GOD is your strength!"
NEHEMIAH 8:10 MSG

❧

"He will yet fill your mouth with
laughter and your lips with shouting."
JOB 8:21 NASB

Joy is the serious business of heaven.

C. S. LEWIS

The trouble with many men is that they
have got just enough religion to make
them miserable. If there is not joy in religion,
you have got a leak in your religion.

BILLY SUNDAY

Let us go singing as far as we go;
the road will be less tedious.

VIRGIL

Happiness is a quiet lover and we don't realize
she has embraced us until she has gone.

BERN WILLIAMS

Throw off your old sinful nature and your former way of life, which is corrupted by lust and deception. Instead, let the Spirit renew your thoughts and attitudes. Put on your new nature, created to be like God—truly righteous and holy.

EPHESIANS 4:22–24 NLT

The key to a great attitude is to rise above your old ways of thinking and start thinking like God thinks. The Bible says we aren't capable of thinking God's actual thoughts. They are too high and holy. But you can think like God—raising your mind-sight to focus on the good, the right, the holy, helping and encouraging others, and ways to express your thankfulness. An attitude is simply a response to what you see—keep your mind tuned in to the good.

Lighthearted Living

Father, there have been many days when I don't
feel like laughing. Work and family life have been
hectic, and I feel I can barely enjoy anything
anymore. Help me experience the joy that You
have already promised me. Don't let me miss out
on one of Your greatest gifts, snuffed out by worry
and fear. Open my eyes to see the moments that
carry with them the carefree smiles and laughter.

*Then was our mouth filled with laughter, and our
tongue with singing: then said they among the
heathen, The Lord hath done great things for them.*
Psalm 126:2 kjv

❧

*A right time to cry and another to laugh,
a right time to lament and another to cheer.*
Ecclesiastes 3:4 msg

❧

But the one who rules in heaven laughs.
Psalm 2:4 nlt

❧

*Be glad in the Lord, and rejoice, ye righteous:
and shout for joy, all ye that are upright in heart.*
Psalm 32:11 kjv

Happiness is like manna; it is to be gathered in grains, and enjoyed every day. It will not keep; it cannot be accumulated; nor have we got to go out of ourselves or into remote places to gather it, since it is rained down from Heaven, at our very doors.

TYRON EDWARDS

God likes a little humor, as evidenced by the fact that he made the monkey, the parrot—and some of you people.

BILLY SUNDAY

Fierce for the right, he bore his part
In strife with many a valiant foe;
But Laughter winged his polished dart,
And kindness tempered every blow.

WILLIAM WINTER

*But let the godly rejoice. Let them be glad in
God's presence. Let them be filled with joy.*
PSALM 68:3 NLT

❧

Many women believe that happiness is a result
of success. "When I find the right person to
marry, I'll be happy." "When I achieve my career
goals. . ." "When I can afford the home I really
want. . ." The truth is that real happiness—
deep inner joy—is the result of living in right
relationship with God rather than the trappings
of success. Regardless of what you may be
facing—good and bad—be happy knowing you
are pleasing your heavenly Father.

Treasures All Around

Lord, I have so many reasons in my life to
be joyful. Remind me each day of the gifts
I've received that I take for granted, such as
my family and friends, earthly possessions,
and good health. I'm truly blessed! And I want
to express my thanksgiving through an attitude
of joy and peace. When I'm tempted to feel
sorry for myself, touch my heart and open
my eyes to the treasures around me.

*Sarah said, God has blessed me with laughter
and all who get the news will laugh with me!*
GENESIS 21:6 MSG

❧

Whoso trusteth in the LORD, happy is he.
PROVERBS 16:20 KJV

❧

*Go then, eat your bread in happiness and
drink your wine with a cheerful heart;
for God has already approved your works.*
ECCLESIASTES 9:7 NASB

❧

A joyful heart is good medicine.
PROVERBS 17:22 NASB

Return on Investment:
Suffering

For it is better, if the will of God be so, that
ye suffer for well doing, than for evil doing.
1 P*ETER* 3:17 KJV

*W*hen Martin Luther was brought before the papal authorities as a heretic, he was asked to recant his beliefs about the Catholic Church. When faced with the possibility of death, he hung his head and asked for twenty-four hours to consider it.

During those hours, Martin Luther chose to walk the difficult road of suffering. He declared, "I cannot and will not recant anything, for to act against our conscience is neither safe for us, nor open to us. On this I take my stand. I can do no other."

Martin Luther did not die that day. He went on to be the father of the Reformation and the first to translate the Bible into the language of the common man.

Life brings difficult circumstances, but not everything that is hard is wrong. Sometimes the right path is less traveled because it isn't easy. Even Jesus Himself had to endure His wilderness experiences. Why do we think we would be exempt? Hebrews 5:8 (NASB) says, "[Jesus] learned obedience from the things which He suffered." Jesus has left us the example that we should learn by our afflictions in humble obedience to God's will. And by experiencing affliction, we can also encounter the healing touch of the Holy Spirit. It is the broken sheep that receives the special attention and loving care of the Shepherd.

*And He went a little beyond them,
and fell on His face and prayed, saying,
"My Father, if it is possible, let this cup pass
from Me; yet not as I will, but as You will."*
MATTHEW 26:39 NASB

❧

*For I reckon that the sufferings of this present
time are not worthy to be compared with
the glory which shall be revealed in us.*
ROMANS 8:18 KJV

❧

*Consider it a sheer gift, friends, when tests and
challenges come at you from all sides. You know
that under pressure, your faith-life is forced into
the open and shows its true colors.*
JAMES 1:2–3 MSG

It's doubtful whether God can bless a
man greatly until He has hurt him deeply.

A. W. TOZER

❧

Ye fearful saints fresh courage take,
The clouds you so much dread
Are big with mercy and shall break,
With blessings on your head.

WILLIAM COWPER

❧

A Christian is someone who shares
the sufferings of God in the world.

DIETRICH BONHOEFFER

❧

Most wretched men
Are cradled into poetry by wrong:
They learn in suffering what they teach in song.

PERCY BYSSHE SHELLEY

Let us run with patience the race that is
set before us, looking unto Jesus the
author and finisher of our faith.
HEBREWS 12:1–2 KJV

Do you ever get tired of life's challenges? Do you
wish you could live a carefree, predictable life?
While that isn't possible, you can have a different
perspective on the challenges that come your way.
The Bible says we will encounter trials in this life.
After all, this world is not our home; it's just a
temporary residence. While we are here, though,
God promised His presence, love, and comfort.
He will walk beside you and give you strength to
overcome whatever is in your path.

The Difficult Path

Father, I know that the right thing to do isn't always the easiest. In those times when I must choose suffering in order to follow You, give me Your peace that surpasses understanding; give me strength to face difficulty; give me Your vision so I can see the future results. I trust You to take care of all my needs no matter how perilous the circumstances. With You, I can do anything.

"Blessed are you when people insult you and persecute you, and falsely say all kinds of evil against you because of Me. Rejoice and be glad, for your reward in heaven is great; for in the same way they persecuted the prophets who were before you."
MATTHEW 5:11–12 NASB

❧

For our present troubles are small and won't last very long. Yet they produce for us a glory that vastly outweighs them and will last forever!
2 CORINTHIANS 4:17 NLT

❧

And ye shall be hated of all men for my name's sake: but he that endureth to the end shall be saved.
MATTHEW 10:22 KJV

I love the man that can smile in trouble, that can gather strength from distress, and grow brave by reflection. 'Tis the business of little minds to shrink; but he whose heart is firm, and whose conscience approves his conduct, will pursue his principles unto death.

THOMAS PAINE

❧

Now let us thank the Eternal Power: convinced
That Heaven but tries our virtue by affliction—
That oft the cloud which wraps the present hour
Serves but to brighten all our future days.

JOHN BROWN

"But as for you, be strong and courageous, for your work will be rewarded."

2 Chronicles 15:7 NLT

What is it that's threatening to make you lose your resolve and give up? Maybe it's exhaustion or discouragement. It might be niggling questions like, "Is this worth it? Is anyone going to notice?" The Bible promises over and over again that your determination will be rewarded. God sees even if no one else does. He understands the process and the difficulty. He will be waiting at the finish line, and your efforts in this life will be well worth it.

❄

A Cross of Prayer

Jesus, thank You for being an example for me
to follow through suffering. While mounted on
a cross in horrific pain, You cried out, "Father,
forgive them." If You can utter those words, how
much more should I pray for those at work and in
my family who persecute me. Help me embrace
the power to live out Your unconditional love
each day no matter what I face.

❄

*Even though you have to put up with
every kind of aggravation in the meantime.
Pure gold put in the fire comes out of it proved
pure; genuine faith put through this suffering
comes out proved genuine. When Jesus wraps this
all up, it's your faith, not your gold, that God
will have on display as evidence of his victory.*

1 PETER 1:6–7 MSG

❧

*Hear the word of the LORD, ye that tremble
at his word; Your brethren that hated you,
that cast you out for my name's sake, said,
Let the LORD be glorified: but he shall appear
to your joy, and they shall be ashamed.*

ISAIAH 66:5 KJV

The Gift of Freedom

There is therefore now no condemnation
to them which are in Christ Jesus.
ROMANS 8:1 KJV

❧

My husband just can't forgive me," Nancy said. "I know what I did was wrong, and I'm sorry. But he keeps bringing it up." You've probably figured out by now that you're not perfect. If you haven't discovered it on your own, someone else will inevitably point it out.

We are all sinners. And sometimes our sin deeply wounds those that we dearly love, often causing bitterness and resentment in that person. You may feel that your loved one won't forgive you and holds you hostage under a long list of wrongdoings. You can't go about your daily life without looming disgrace over your soul, always pressured by the expectation to pay back enough to make up for your offenses.

There is a place for remorse, resulting in change for each of us. But the feelings of condemnation, however, do not come from God. Jesus came so that you no longer have to live under the guilt and shame of your sins. Even when men and women won't forgive, God does. Embrace the gift of forgiveness that God has given you, and don't let bitter people take it from you.

Colossians 1:14 (KJV) says, "In [Christ] we have redemption through his blood, even the forgiveness of sins." You can live in freedom knowing that in Christ alone your debts have been paid, no matter how great or small your sin. Believe it and live free.

The Spirit of the Sovereign Lord *is upon me,
for the* Lord *has anointed me to bring good
news to the poor. He has sent me to comfort the
brokenhearted and to proclaim that captives
will be released and prisoners will be freed.*

Isaiah 61:1 nlt

*And ye shall know the truth,
and the truth shall make you free.*

John 8:32 kjv

*"Everyone who believes in him is
declared right with God—something
the law of Moses could never do."*

Acts 13:39 nlt

150

O Lamb of God! 'tis joy to know
That path is o'er of shame and woe,
For us so meekly trod.
JAMES GEORGE DECK

A man should never be ashamed to own
he has been in the wrong, which is but
saying in other words that he is wiser
today than he was yesterday.
ALEXANDER POPE

But the soul renounced shall abide in the
boundlessness of God's life. This is liberty, this is
prosperity. The more we lose, the more we gain.
WATCHMAN NEE

"I have forgiven you for all that you have done,"
the Lord God declares.

EZEKIEL 16:63 NASB

You are forgiven. No matter what you've done. No matter how or when or what—God's forgiveness is waiting for you. The moment you acknowledge your sin and ask to be forgiven, it's done. Strangely, that may be difficult for you to accept. You may feel you must make your own atonement. But it's a feat you will never accomplish. Only God's perfect Son was able to do the job. Abandon your pride and receive His forgiveness. Don't wait another moment.

❧

Living in Grace

Lord, there are days when I feel burdened by guilt from my past, but I know Your Word says I am forgiven. Help me today to live with a clean conscience knowing that the sacrifice of Your Son paid the price for all my sins. Give me grace to deal with the pressure from others who still try to punish me with their words and hurtful attitudes.

❧

This is a covenant not of written laws, but of the Spirit. The old written covenant ends in death; but under the new covenant, the Spirit gives life.
2 Corinthians 3:6 NLT

❧

But one who looks intently at the perfect law, the law of liberty, and abides by it, not having become a forgetful hearer but an effectual doer, this man will be blessed in what he does.
James 1:25 NASB

❧

Now the Lord is the Spirit, and where the Spirit of the Lord is, there is liberty.
2 Corinthians 3:17 NASB

Either sin is with you, lying on your shoulders, or it is lying on Christ, the Lamb of God. Now if it is lying on your back, you are lost; but if it is resting on Christ, you are free, and you will be saved. Now choose what you want.

MARTIN LUTHER

❧

A forgiveness ought to be like a canceled note, torn in two and burned up, so that it can never be shown against the man.

HENRY WARD BEECHER

❧

Compassion costs. It is easy enough to argue, criticize, and condemn, but redemption is costly, and comfort draws from the deep. Brains can argue, but it takes heart to comfort.

SAMUEL CHADWICK

But by the grace of God I am what I am: and his
grace which was bestowed upon me was not in vain;
but I laboured more abundantly than they all:
yet not I, but the grace of God which was with me.
1 Corinthians 15:10 kjv

Grace is often defined as God's unmerited favor.
It means that His love for us, His care, and His
concern are all free gifts—we haven't earned them.
What a wonderful thing to be loved and accepted—
just because! In God's eyes, you are already pretty
enough, smart enough, good enough to receive
His best. He loves you for yourself. He wants you
to become all you were created to be, but your
relationship with Him doesn't hinge on it.
What a wonderful word "grace" is!

Great Forgiveness

Father, I often receive painful comments from people in my life that can't let go of a previous grievance. As much as I understand their bitterness, I'm starting to feel my own resentment. It would be so easy to start holding a set of grudges of my own, so help me to forgive as I am forgiven. I don't want their sin to make me guilty of the same.

For all have sinned, and come short of the glory of God; being justified freely by his grace through the redemption that is in Christ Jesus.
ROMANS 3:23–24 KJV

Christ has set us free to live a free life. So take your stand! Never again let anyone put a harness of slavery on you.
GALATIANS 5:1 MSG

When we trust in him, we're free to say whatever needs to be said, bold to go wherever we need to go.
EPHESIANS 3:12 MSG

Beautiful Memories

Watch yourself, that you do not forget.
DEUTERONOMY 6:12 NASB

❧

*P*uritan minister Richard Steele once wrote, "The soul of man is a subject of wonder; and nothing more wonderful than the memory." Memories have the ability to shame or to heal, but when you allow them to wash over your soul through the lens of God's grace, they can minister to you in a moving way.

Reflection on the past—good or bad—under the cleansing wash of redemption will give you perspective for the future. Bad choices become a way to caution and teach. Good choices can bring about rejoicing and thanksgiving. Either way, there is power in remembering.

Many times in the Old Testament God instructs the children of Israel not to forget. He often told them to set up stones to memorialize a location where certain miracles occurred and even gave those places a name. But over and over, the people forgot the works of God and repeated the same mistakes.

Today, take time to reflect on all God has done in your life through the good and even hard times. For the blessings, rejoice! And for those memories of shame, remember the promise of Christ to cleanse us from all unrighteousness and to set you free from the guilt that binds you. Then make a new memory—the day you were released from those chains. What a blessing to look back over your life and draw a beautiful portrait of God's redeeming power!

*"Always remember this day. This is the day when you came out of Egypt from a house of slavery. G*OD *brought you out of here with a powerful hand."*
EXODUS 13:3 MSG

❧

*Remember now thy Creator
in the days of thy youth.*
ECCLESIASTES 12:1 KJV

❧

Then in that day the nations will resort to the root of Jesse, who will stand as a signal for the peoples; and His resting place will be glorious.
ISAIAH 11:10 NASB

I sit beside my lonely fire
And pray for wisdom yet:
For calmness to remember
Or courage to forget.

CHARLES HAMILTON AÏDÉ

❦

How cruelly sweet are the echoes that start
When memory plays an old tune on the heart!

ELIZA COOK

❦

Christian, remember the goodness
of God in the frost of adversity.

CHARLES SPURGEON

❦

Friends depart, and memory takes
them to her caverns, pure and deep.

THOMAS HAYNES BAYLY

The life of the godly is full of light and joy.
PROVERBS 13:9 NLT

When your life is hid in the goodness of God,
your possibilities are limitless. Your future is
more than bright—it's dazzling. If you are at the
beginning of your walk with God, you are a
fortunate woman. The road ahead may not be
easy, but it will be the greatest adventure, the
greatest race you've ever attempted. And best of
all, the destination is certain. Throw yourself
unreservedly into the work that God has called
you to. Take hold of your future with both hands.

Blessed Recollections

Father, I'm thankful for all the blessings I can see throughout the memories of my life. You have given me so much—family, friends, a comfortable home, and most of all the Good News of Your Son, Jesus Christ. Help me understand how the tragedies and pain throughout the years have brought about Your good and given me the peace to receive Your forgiveness for my failures.

*If the Son therefore shall make you free,
ye shall be free indeed.*
JOHN 8:36 KJV

❧

*Remember the world of wonders he has made,
his miracles, and the verdicts he's rendered.*
PSALM 105:5 MSG

❧

*And now, dear brothers and sisters, one final
thing. Fix your thoughts on what is true,
and honorable, and right, and pure, and
lovely, and admirable. Think about things that
are excellent and worthy of praise.*
PHILIPPIANS 4:8 NLT

Sad soul, take comfort, nor forget
that sunrise never failed us yet.
CELIA THAXTER

❧

I cannot but remember such things were,
That were most precious to me.
WILLIAM SHAKESPEARE

❧

Oh, I have roamed o'er many lands,
And many friends I've met;
Not one fair scene or kindly smile
Can this fond heart forget.
THOMAS HAYNES BAYLY

❧

Those who cannot remember the
past are condemned to repeat it.
GEORGE SANTAYANA

Instruct the wise, and they will be even wiser.
PROVERBS 9:9 NLT

The number one characteristic of the unrighteous is their inability to learn. They make the same mistakes over and over, never recognizing their error or understanding that they have been given the power to change. You have seen the error of your ways and turned to God. Now continue to learn, continue to change, and continue to grow in the image of your heavenly Father. He is proud of your progress in righteousness.

Dark Made Light

Dear God, oftentimes remembering the past makes me feel overwhelmingly ashamed. It's hard for me to believe that You have forgiven me for some of my worst mistakes. Wash over me with Your grace and peace, reminding me that the work of Jesus was to free me from the darkest of deeds. I no longer need to live under the burden of shame. Help me embrace Your freedom.

Bless the LORD, O my soul,
and forget none of His benefits.
PSALM 103:2 NASB

I will remember the works of the LORD:
surely I will remember thy wonders of old.
PSALM 77:11 KJV

Therefore, brethren, stand fast,
and hold the traditions which ye have
been taught, whether by word, or our epistle.
2 THESSALONIANS 2:15 KJV

Delightful Rest

Rest in the LORD, and wait patiently for him.
PSALM 37:7 KJV

❧

*O*ur nation brims with creative, hardworking people who achieve unbelievable accomplishments. But one skill we lack—the ability to rest. We already take less than half of the days the rest of the developed world enjoys.

Americans work long hours, often multiple jobs at once, and then overwhelm free time with activities. As a result, we suffer the physical and mental consequences of stress and anxiety. That's why the Bible commands us to rest, not as some ritualistic duty, but rather a delight of both body and soul.

God Himself was the original partaker of a day of respite. He created the whole world in six days, and on the seventh, He rested. If God needs time out from His work, so do we.

Blaise Pascal once said, "All of man's troubles stem from his inability to sit quietly in a room alone." Have you ever tried to dress an anxious child or wash a hyper dog? It's not easy! In order to accomplish the goal, you must first reach calm. In the same way, it is in times of peace and tranquility that our minds and hearts can be cared for by the Holy Spirit to both cleanse with conviction and strengthen with prayer and the Word.

"Stop at the crossroads and look around.
Ask for the old, godly way, and walk in it. Travel
its path, and you will find rest for your souls."
JEREMIAH 6:16 NLT

❧

"Remember the sabbath day, to keep it holy."
EXODUS 20:8 NASB

❧

Take my yoke upon you, and learn of me;
for I am meek and lowly in heart:
and ye shall find rest unto your souls.
MATTHEW 11:29 KJV

Thou hast made us for Thyself, O Lord;
and our heart is restless until it rests in Thee.

AUGUSTINE

Never, never did Christ send a heavy laden
one to work; never, never did He send a hungry
one, a weary one, a sick or sorrowing one, away
on any service. For such the Bible only says,
Come, come, come.

HUDSON TAYLOR

That blessed mood,
In which the burden of the mystery,
In which the heavy and the weary weight
Of all this unintelligible world,
Is lightened.

WILLIAM WORDSWORTH

The beloved of the L<small>ORD</small> shall dwell in safety by him; and the Lord shall cover him all the day long, and he shall dwell between his shoulders.
D<small>EUTERONOMY</small> 33:12 <small>KJV</small>

When you think of rest—you probably think of a nap or picture yourself soaking in a tub. While you need physical rest, God wants your soul well rested and full of His presence as well. Read encouraging scriptures that build your faith. Spend time with Him in prayer. You'll feel like you've had a spiritual power nap. You'll come away rested and strengthened in your soul, safe from the assaults of the day.

Foundation of Peace

Father, my life can seem out of control at times, almost like an endless cycle from one place to the next. If I'm not working, I'm volunteering for extracurricular activities or keeping up with chores. I don't feel like I could make time to rest, even when I desperately want to! Remind me to enjoy times of calm so that I can find my strength in You.

Let my soul be at rest again,
for the LORD has been good to me.
PSALM 116:7 NLT

❧

[God] said before,
"This is the time and place to rest,
to give rest to the weary.
This is the place to lay down your burden."
But they won't listen.
ISAIAH 28:12 MSG

❧

For in six days the LORD made the heavens and
the earth, the sea and all that is in them, and
rested on the seventh day; therefore the LORD
blessed the sabbath day and made it holy.
EXODUS 20:11 NASB

Rest and be thankful.
WILLIAM WORDSWORTH

❦

O bed! O bed! delicious bed!
That heaven upon earth to the weary head!
THOMAS HOOD

❦

If we would sanctify the Sabbath acceptably,
we must call the Sabbath "a delight."
THOMAS CASE

*"Come to Me, all who are weary
and heavy-laden, and I will give you rest."*
MATTHEW 11:28 NASB

───────── ❧ ─────────

Weary. Burdened. Need rest. Those words read
like a repeating entry in a woman's daily journal.
Most women feel they've earned the right to be
burdened. What else but weary could they be with
all they have to do? Jesus said that He would give
rest to those who are weary. He would lighten our
loads. Take one burden at a time and hand it over
to Him. And then rest in the peace that Jesus
has our lives in the palm of His hands.

Worthy Investment

Lord, I know that I've been too busy to spend quality time with You. Give me the wisdom to prioritize my life and decide what I can remove. I realize that a change in my schedule will disappoint some, so give me grace as I deal with hurt feelings and frustrations. But making time for You is an investment that will change me for the better and positively affect everyone around me.

It is useless for you to work so hard
from early morning until late at night,
anxiously working for food to eat;
for God gives rest to his loved ones.
PSALM 127:2 NLT

The fear of the LORD leads to life, so that
one may sleep satisfied, untouched by evil.
PROVERBS 19:23 NASB

He maketh me to lie down in green
pastures: he leadeth me beside the
still waters. He restoreth my soul.
PSALM 23:2–3 KJV

The Seeds of
Second Chances

Therefore if any man be in Christ,
he is a new creature: old things are passed
away; behold, all things are become new.

2 CORINTHIANS 5:17 KJV

*L*aura just wanted to be loved. And her life was changed forever when she discovered her pregnancy. It was difficult for many years being a single mom, but it was through Laura's situation that she developed a passion to help other young women, ministering to both their physical and spiritual needs, a calling that would not have taken place without the pain of her own sin.

One of the most beautiful gifts of the Christian faith is the ability to start over, no matter what iniquities we may have committed. Under the grace of Jesus it is never too late to change and follow God's will even through the mistakes. Through God's redemptive power, He takes the rotten leftovers of our past and uses them to fertilize the soil of His future purposes.

Rahab, a prostitute in the city of Jericho, understood second chances. Despite being a harlot and the daughter of a pagan people, Rahab believed in the God of Israel and helped the Israelites conquer the city. This former woman of the night converted to Judaism and became an ancestor of Jesus Christ Himself.

There is no sin too great for God to forgive, no soul too lost to be found. No matter how far away you have found yourself from the Father, He can turn your shame into glory.

It is a mistake to suppose that people
succeed through success; they often
succeed through failures.

UNKNOWN

When it is dark enough, you can see the stars.

RALPH WALDO EMERSON

We must always change, renew, rejuvenate
ourselves, otherwise we harden.

JOHANN WOLFGANG VON GOETHE

Free grace can go into the gutter,
and bring up a jewel!

CHARLES SPURGEON

Blanket of Mercy

God, I'm grateful that no matter what I've done,
Your grace covers my sin. I'm sorry for the times
I've failed to do the right thing, but I'm in awe each
time You take the shame from the past and use
it to bring Your glory. I'm honored to reflect the
testimony that the God of the Bible brings forth
light from darkness. Your grace is truly amazing!

*"Forget about what's happened; don't keep
going over old history. Be alert, be present.
I'm about to do something brand-new."*
ISAIAH 43:19 MSG

*You have turned my mourning into joyful
dancing. You have taken away my clothes
of mourning and clothed me with joy.*
PSALM 30:11 NLT

*Come now, and let us reason together, saith
the LORD: though your sins be as scarlet, they
shall be as white as snow; though they be
red like crimson, they shall be as wool.*
ISAIAH 1:18 KJV

Smooth seas do not make skillful sailors.

 AFRICAN PROVERB

❧

Beauty for ashes God hath decreed!
Help He provideth for ev'ry need;
What is unlovely He will restore;
Grace all-sufficient: What need we more?

GRANT COLFAX TULLAR

❧

We acquire the strength we have overcome.

RALPH WALDO EMERSON

❧

He rides pleasantly enough
whom the grace of God carries.

THOMAS À KEMPIS

*"I will give you a new heart,
and I will put a new spirit in you."*
EZEKIEL 36:26 NLT

Some of the most surprising news about God's
presence is that He does more than fix you up
the best He can and send you on your way—
somehow He makes you brand-new. His offer
of new life is one of the few truly fresh starts
you can experience. Sure, He doesn't delete
the consequences that still have to be battled
through—but He does have the power to change
your heart and help you manage those
consequences. Ask Him to make you new.

＊

Ministry of Redemption

Father, as I evaluate the struggles I've had in
the past and the healing I've found, I want to
know how You can use my experiences to help
others. Will You show me a ministry that I can
participate in to comfort women like me and
show them how to find their hope in Christ?
More than anything, I want the pain of my past
to bring hope to someone who needs it.

＊

Weeping may last for the night,
but a shout of joy comes in the morning.
PSALM 30:5 NASB